Coloring Book

ANIMALS

of

North America

Mark Shawe

Book Series: Animal Planet

In this Coloring Book you will find:

- 20 original realistic full-page images of wild animals of North America on single-sided sheets to prevent bleed-through
- 60 interesting unusual facts about the animals

Grab you favorite tool: pencils, crayons, markers or paints, and start coloring!

ISBN: 9781079225525

WORLD MAP

American buffalo

Despite the fact that occasionally called a bison, the American buffalo is not identified with the wild oxen on the planet. It is more firmly identified with dairy animals and goats. Buffalos spend a lot of time eating. They start the day by having a two-hour meal and after resting for a while they go find a new place to start eating again. They also drink water on a daily basis, and if they are in colder regions, they consume snow. Buffalos are constantly moving. During summer they always travel, and it is estimated that they usually travel 3.2 km daily. They choose the places they go depending on the variety of vegetation, water availability, and the number of insects

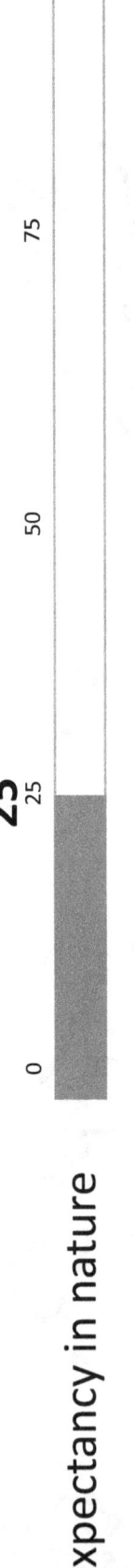

life expectancy in nature

weigh up to   1150 kg (2535 lb)

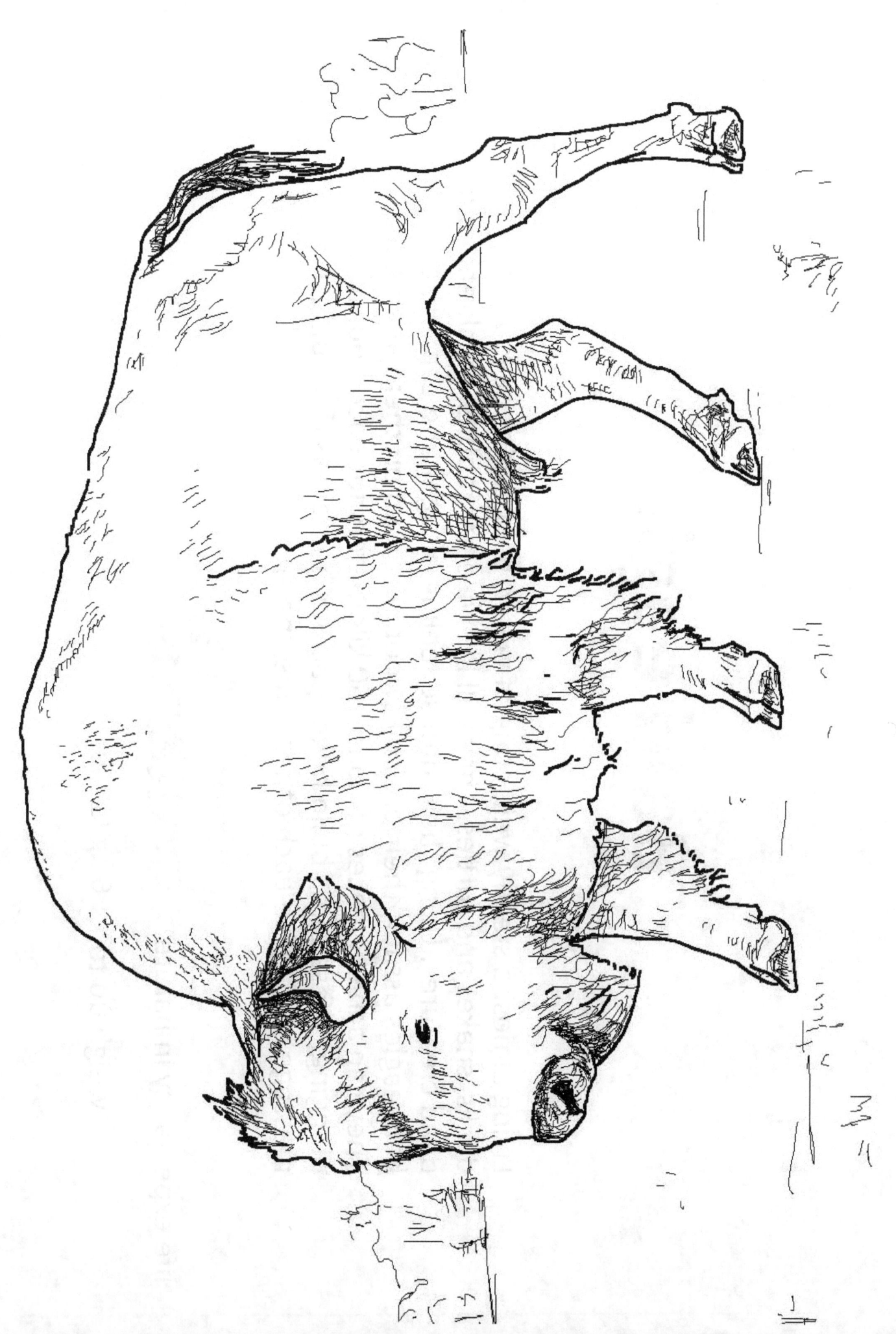

Bald eagle

Living almost a steady wellspring of water, bald eagles devour fish, ducks, snakes and turtles. They will likewise eat rabbits, muskrats, and dead creatures. Using their intense feeling of sight and capable claws, bald eagles assault their prey by swooping down on them at an edge. They can achieve paces of up to 160 kilometers for each hour when plunging. These birds build huge spacious homes, as if sending a message to us: give each other some space!

life expectancy in nature

| 0 | 25 | **28** | 50 | 75 | 100 |

weigh up to   6 kg (13 lb)

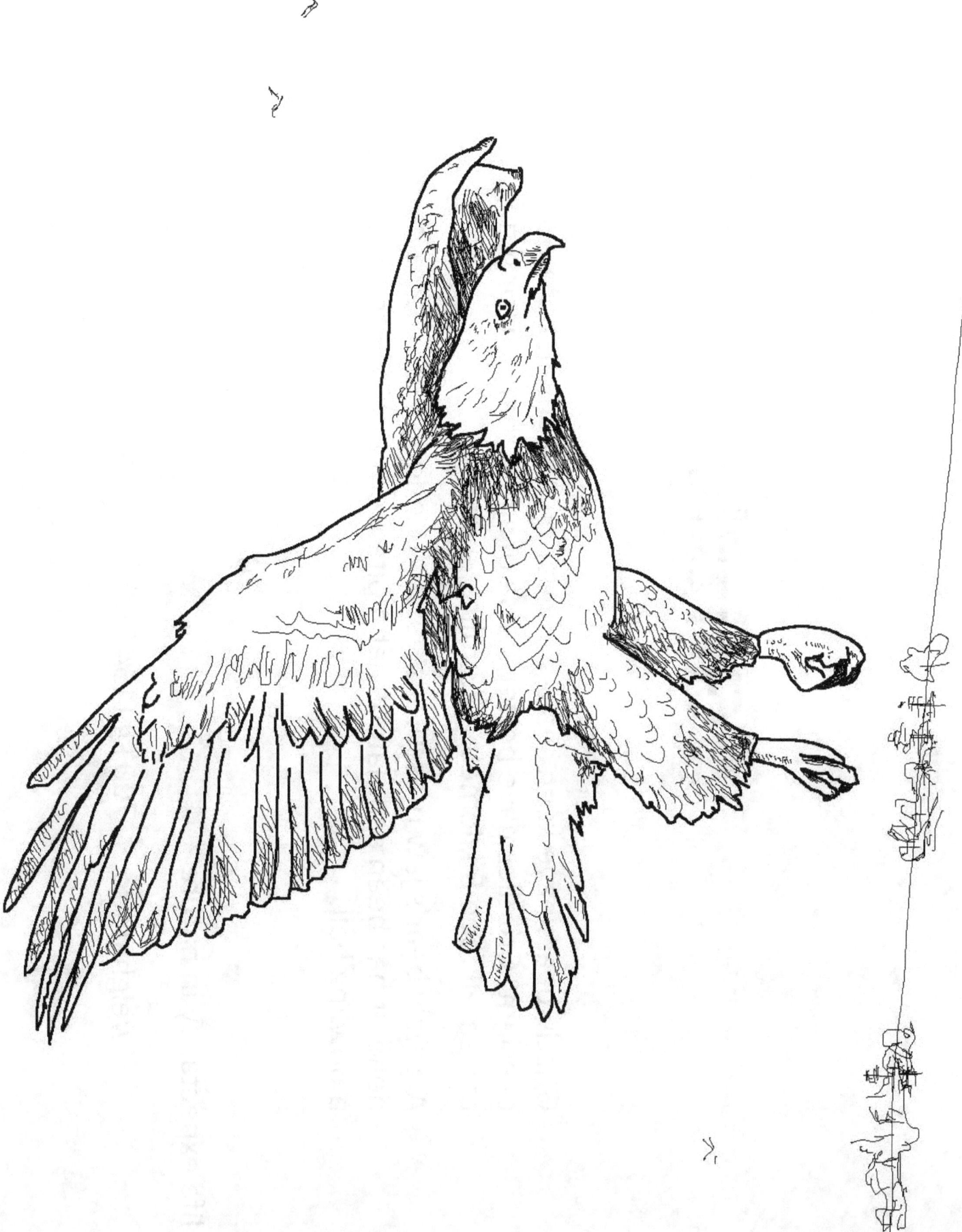

Grizzly

Grizzly bears have keen senses of hearing and smell, but poor eyesight. Grizzlies have better sense of smell than a hound dog. They can smell food 5 kilometers (3 miles) away.

A grizzly bear's jaw pressure is powerful enough to crush a human head. It has been estimated that a bite from a grizzly could even crush a bowling ball.

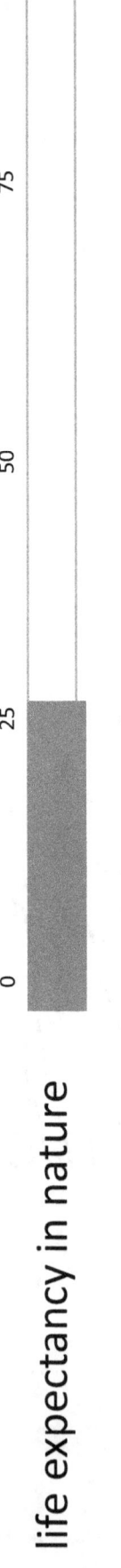

life expectancy in nature

weigh up to   700 kg (1545 lb)

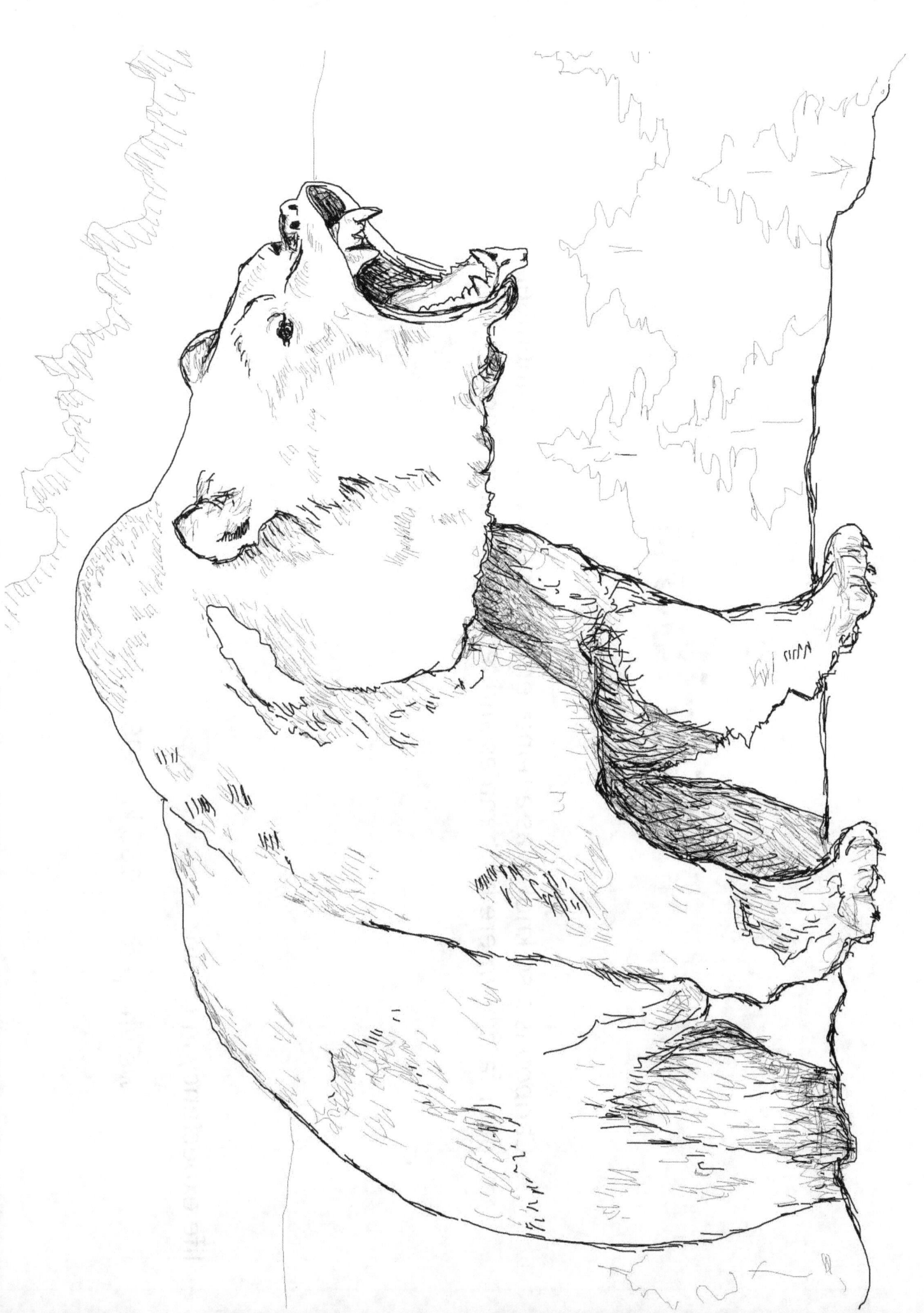

Caribou

Caribou is also known as a reindeer. Caribou is the only member of deer family where both males and females wear antlers.

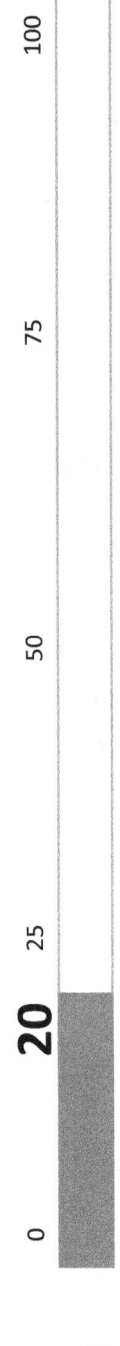

life expectancy in nature

0   20   25   50   75   100

weigh up to   180 kg (396 lb)

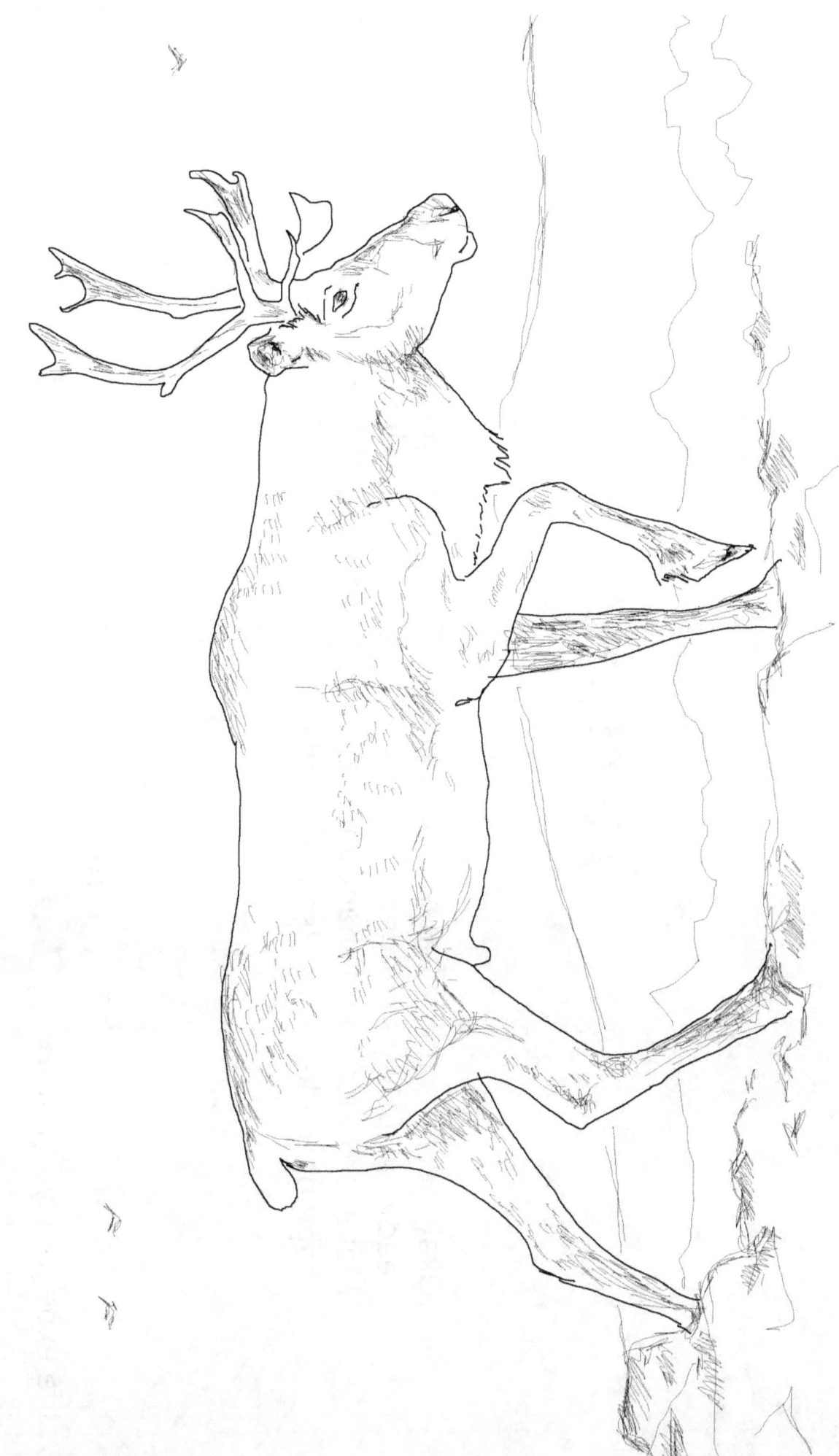

Turkey

Okay, here's a really fun fact to brag about in front of your class.
Ready? A turkey's gender can be determined from its droppings.
Males produce spiral shaped feces while females have feces in the
shape of the letter "J." Isn't that cute?

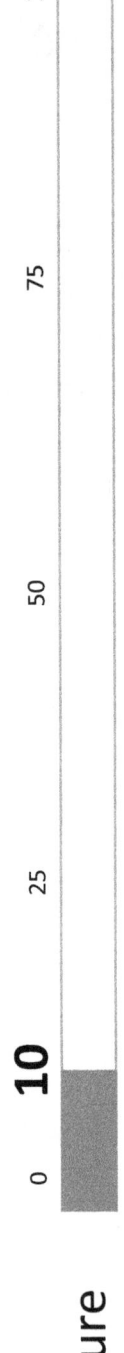

| 0 | **10** | 25 | 50 | 75 | 100 |

life expectancy in nature

weigh up to   5 kg (11 lb)

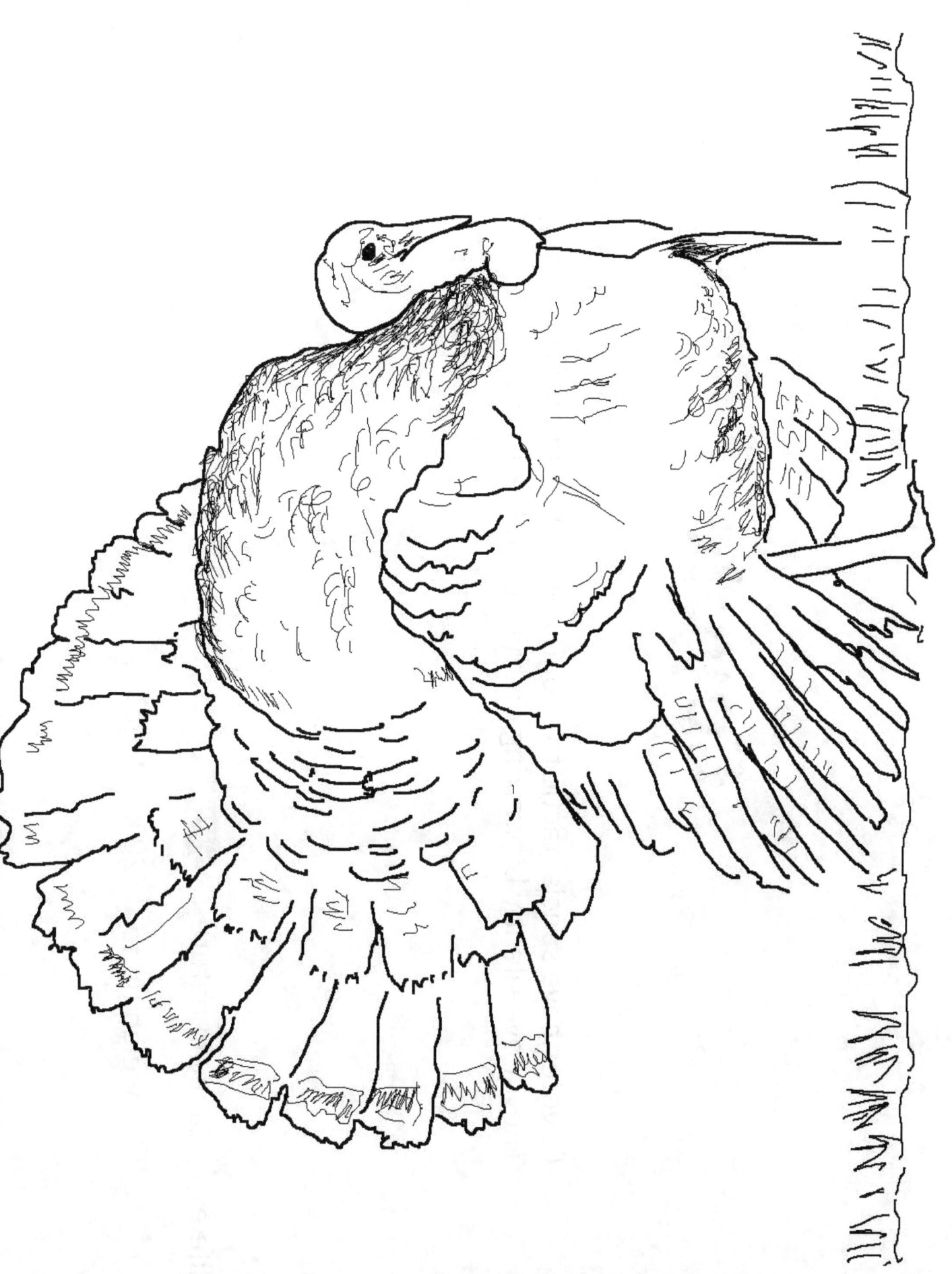

Coyote

Coyotes have special tactic to avoid predators and potential danger. They move silently by walking on the tips of their toes.

life expectancy in nature

0　**10**　25　50　75　100

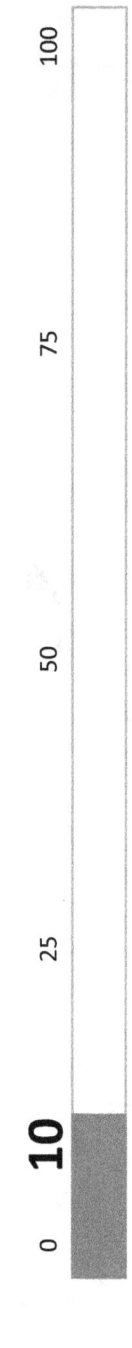

weigh up to　20 kg (44 lb)

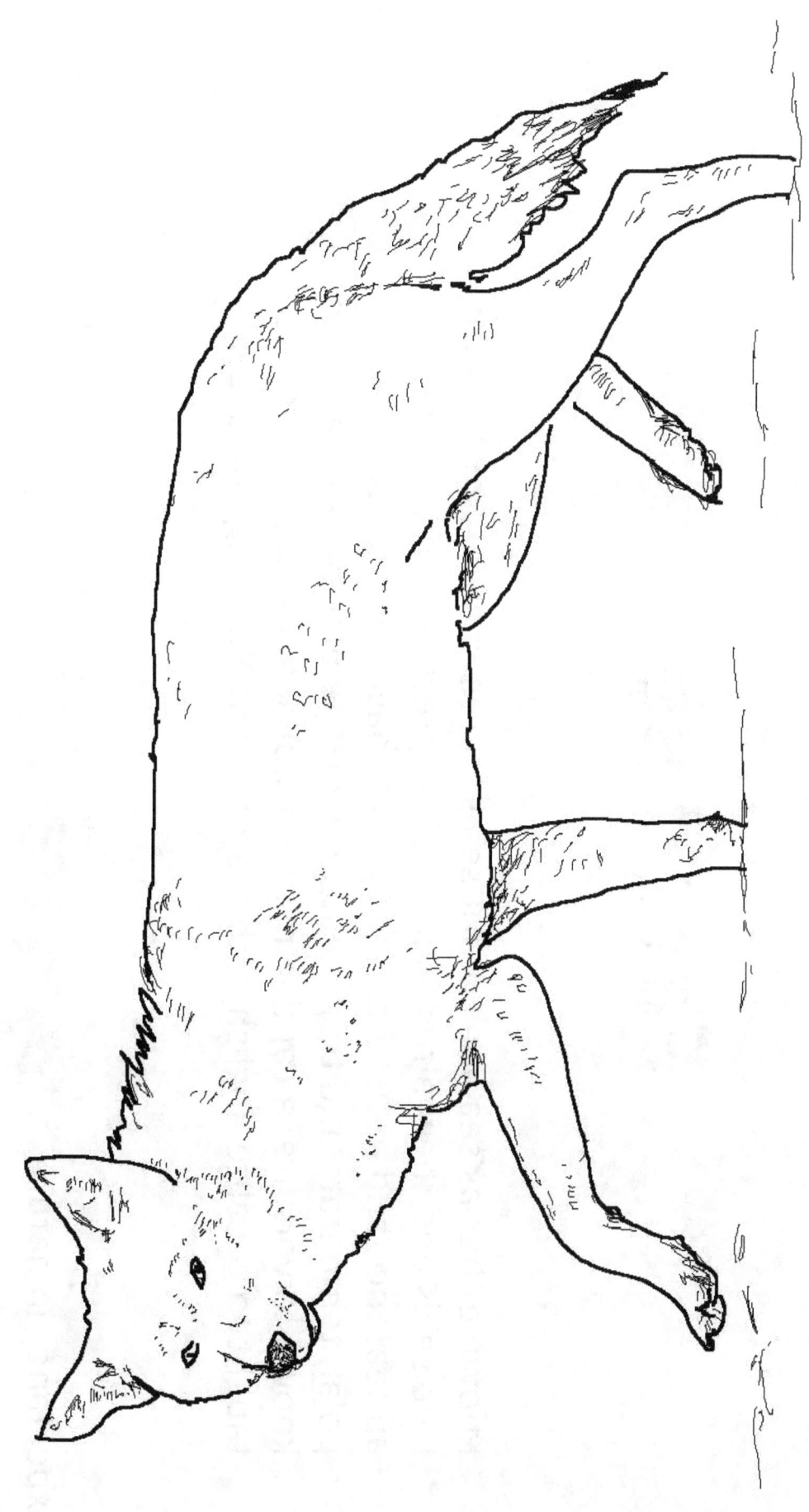

Eared seal

Known either as sea lions or fur seals, eared seals are distinct from true seals and the walrus. With their expressive eyes, furry appearance and natural curiosity, seals have a wide appeal. Native to polar, temperate and tropical waters on the planet, seals are also known to vocalize: a captive male harbor seal named Hoover was taught to vocalize English with a prominent New England accent.

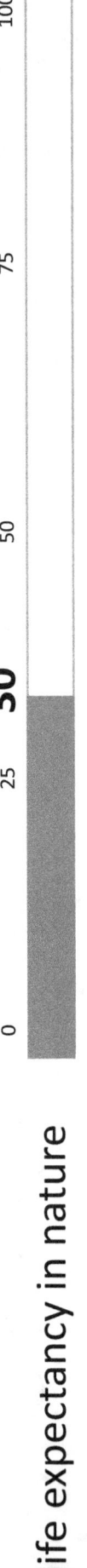

life expectancy in nature

| 0 | 25 | **30** | 50 | 75 | 100 |

weigh up to   700 kg (1550 lb)

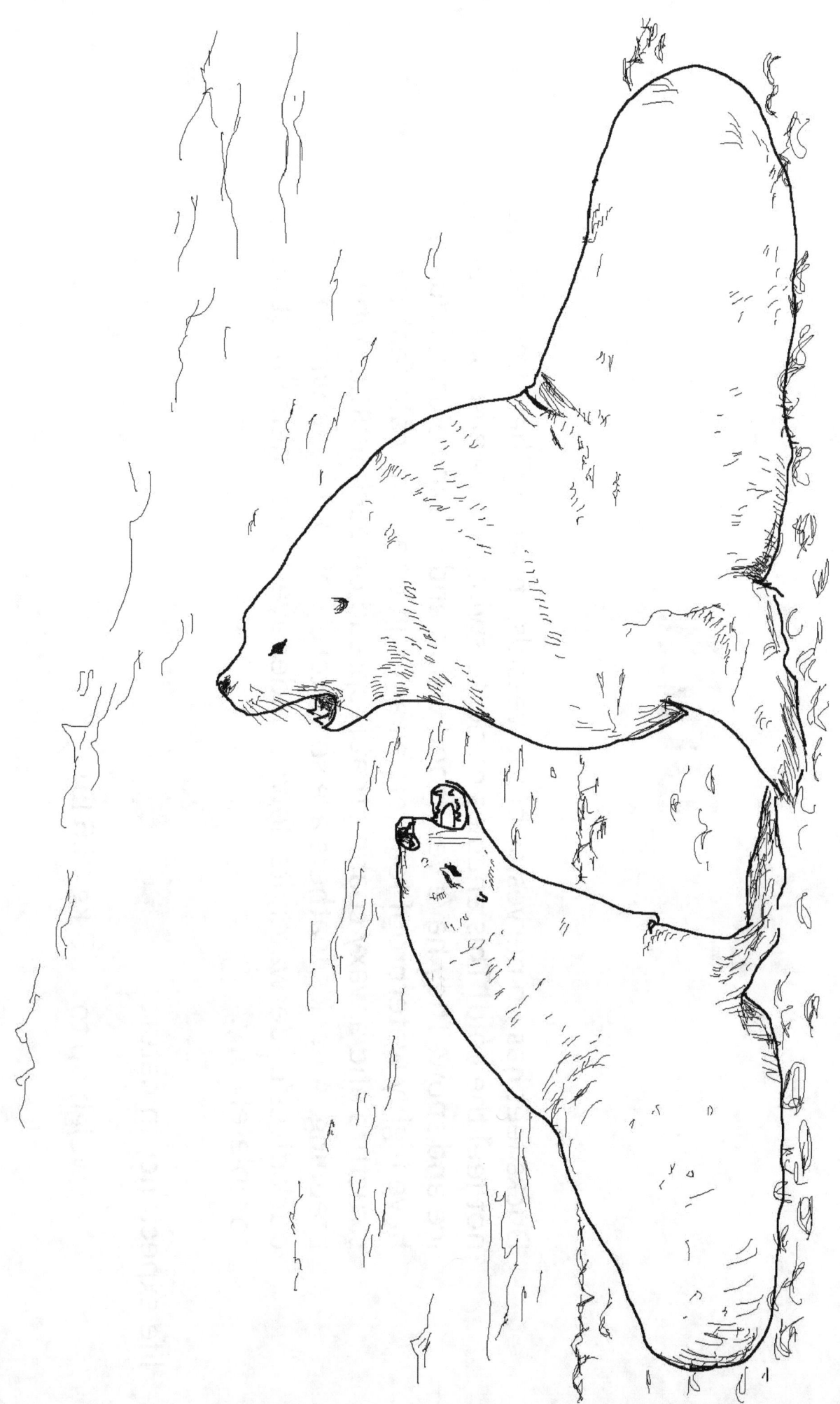

Duck

Ducks feet has no nerves or blood vessels, meaning that their feet do not feel the cold! This enables ducks to swim in icy water, and walk in ice and snow. They have very good vision and see in color. All ducks have highly waterproof feathers as a result of an intricate feather structure and a waxy coating that is spread on each feather while preening. A duck's feathers are so waterproof that even when the duck dives underwater, its downy underlayer of feathers will stay completely dry.

life expectancy in nature

0   **20**   25   50   75   100

weigh up to   3 kg (6,6 lb)

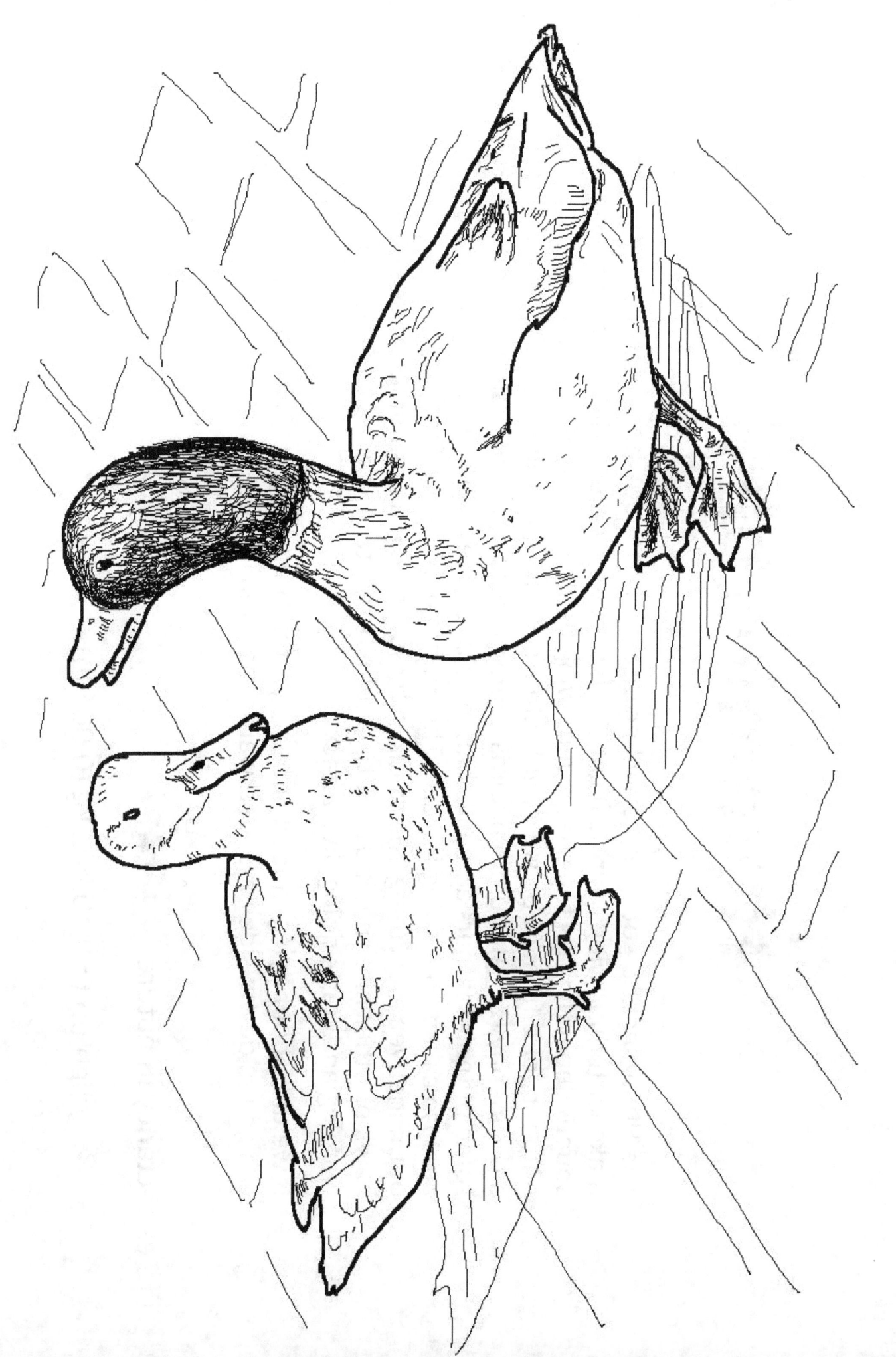

Hummingbird

The Hummingbird got their name because of the unique humming sound they make with their wings during flight. Each species creates a different humming sound, depending on the speed of its wing beats. The smallest is the bee hummingbird from Cuba is 5 centimeters (2 inches) tall and weighing less than a U.S. penny (2.5 g). Hummingbirds come in all colors of the rainbow, and some of their feathers actually change color as they move in the light, so they are also called "the flying jewels". The hummingbirds are fearless, as they can outmaneuver everything unless taken by surprise. If a hummingbird sees a hawk or other bird that it doesn't want in its territory, it gives a high-pitched warning and starts doing dive attacks.

If we talk about flying, nobody does it better. Hummingbird is like helicopter, can go up, down, sideways, backward, and even upside down!

life expectancy in nature

| 0 | **9** | 25 | 50 | 75 | 100 |

weigh up to   0,002 kg (0,004 lb)

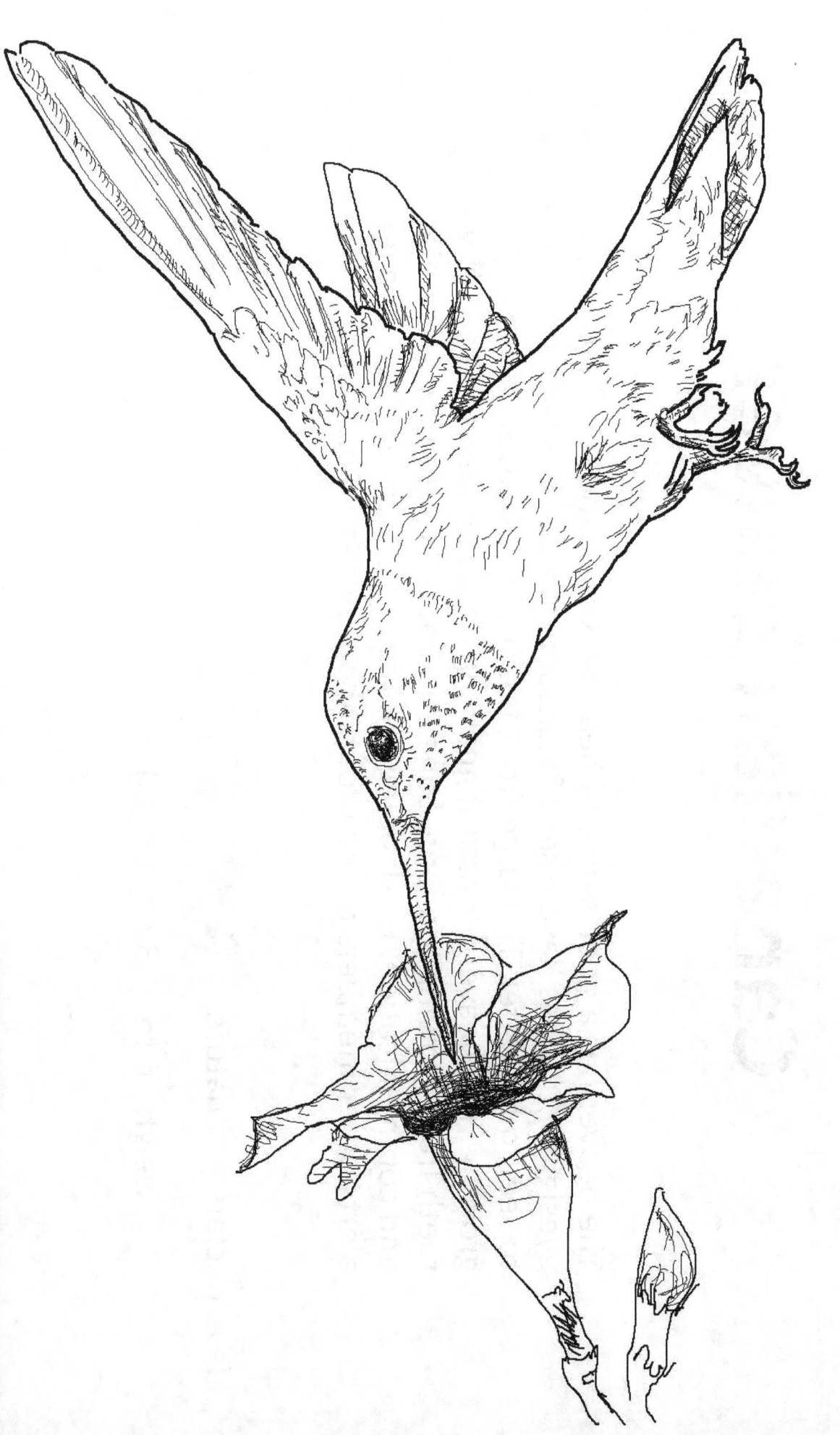

Canadian beaver

The beaver has a good sense of hearing, smell, and touch. It has poor eyesight, but does have a set of transparent eyelids which allow them to see under water. The large front teeth of the beaver never stop growing. The beavers constant gnawing on wood helps to keep their teeth from growing too long. Long and flat tail is used for swimming and communication. By slapping the water surface with tail, beaver alerts other members of the group about potential danger.

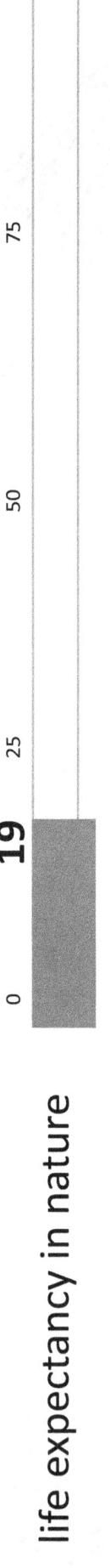

life expectancy in nature

19

0   25   50   75   100

weigh up to   32 kg (70 lb)

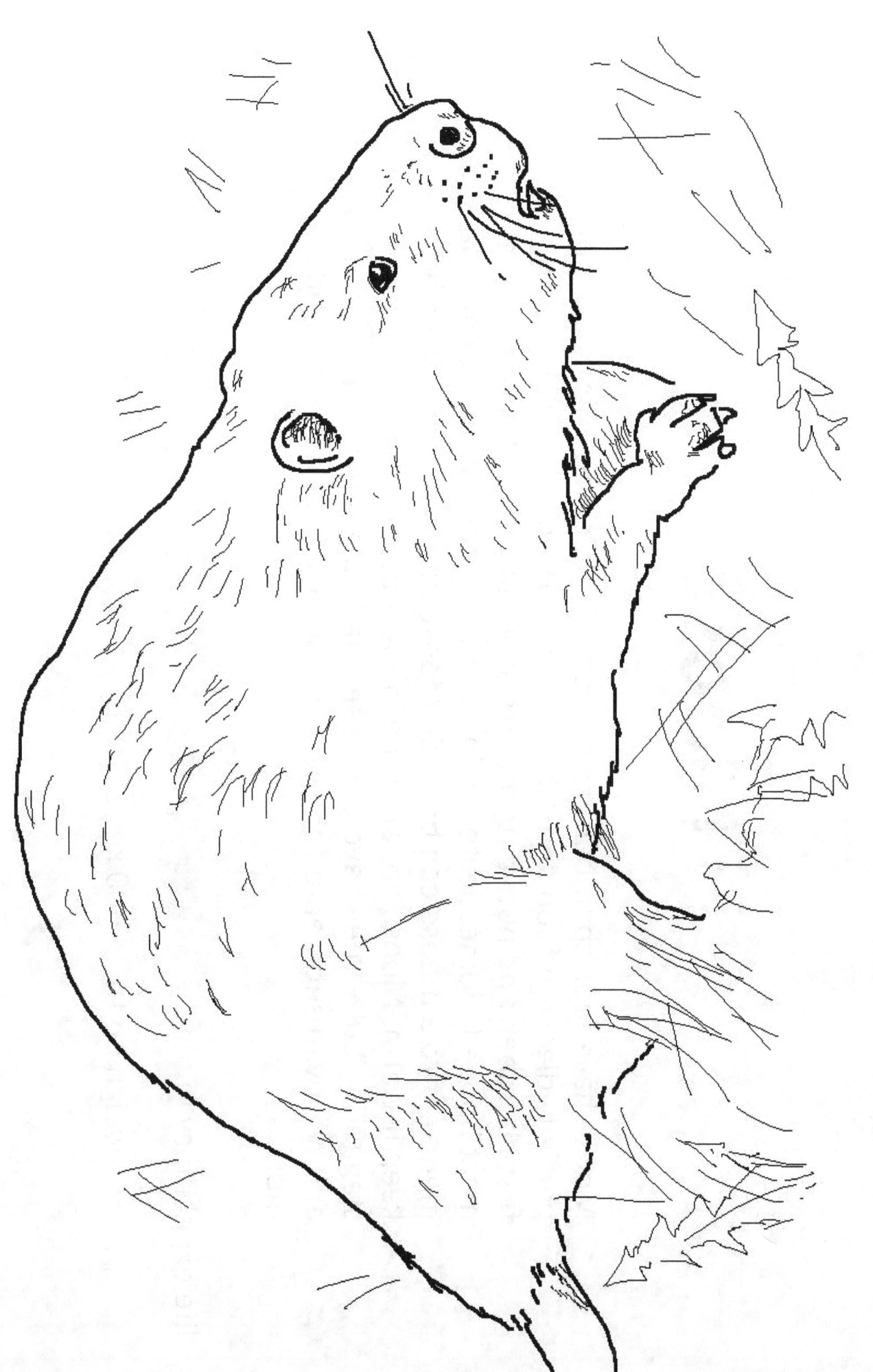

Moose

Moose have four-chambered stomachs, as do cows. They regurgitate partially digested food and "chew their cud". Food is fermented in the first chamber, and nutrients are extracted in the next three. Unlike most hooved, domesticated animals, moose cannot digest hay, and feeding it to a moose can be fatal. Moose hair is hollow, which helps keep it warm. Moose are at home in the water despite their staggering bulk. They have been seen paddling several miles at a time, and will even submerge completely, staying under for 30 seconds or more.

life expectancy in nature

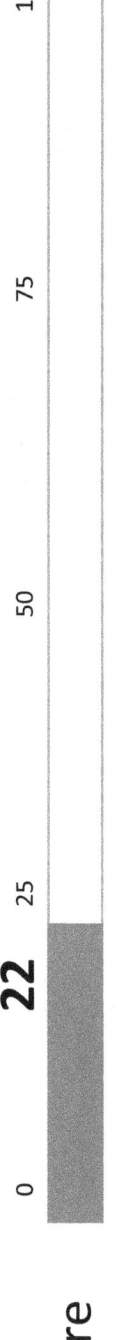

0   **22** 25   50   75   100

weigh up to   600 kg (1320 lb)

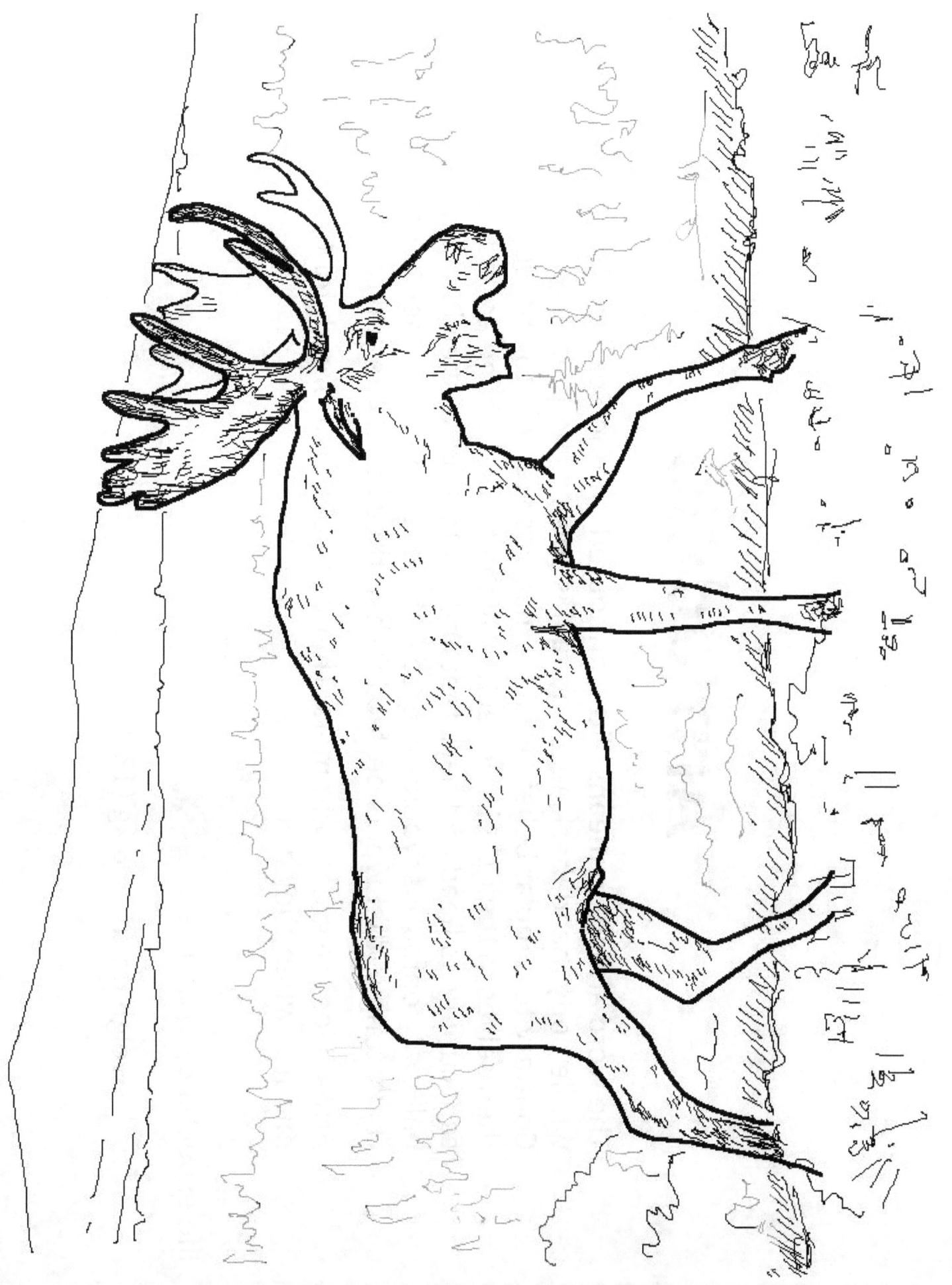

Armadillo

The word armadillo means "little armoured one" in Spanish. Their whole body (head, back, legs and tail) is covered with bony plates. Contrary to popular belief, not all armadillos are able to encase themselves in their shells. In fact, only the three-banded armadillo can, curling its head and back feet and contorting its shell into a hard ball that confounds would-be predators. Like anteaters, they have long sticky tongue that works perfectly when they hunt ants and termites.

Armadillos are great swimmers. They can hold their breath for 6 minutes when they dive.

life expectancy in nature

0   4   25   50   75   100

weigh up to   6 kg (13 lb)

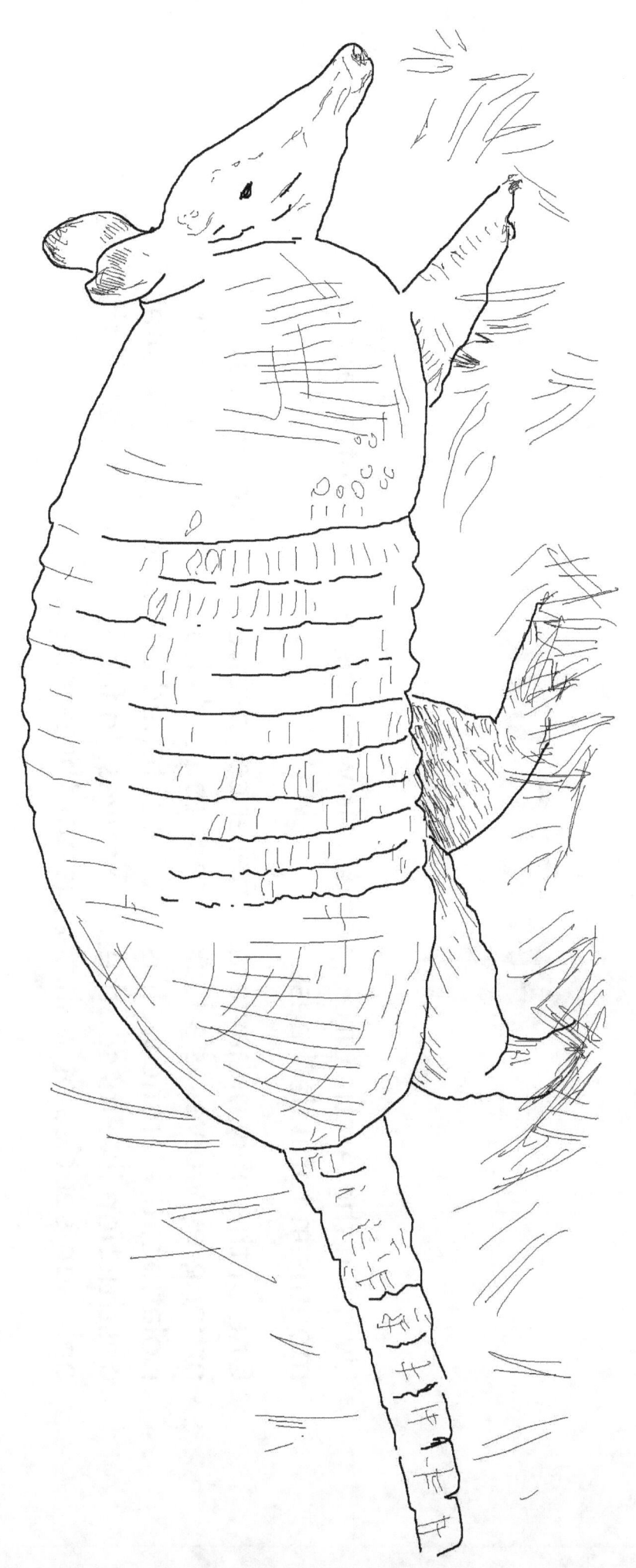

Arctic wolf

Living in the Arctic Circle, the Arctic wolf spends five out of twelve months in total darkness.

One of the only behavioral differences between arctic wolves and other grey wolves is a lack of fear towards humans. Thanks to its isolation, the arctic wolf is not threatened by hunting and habitat destruction like its southern relatives. In fact, the arctic wolf is the only sub-species of wolf that is not threatened.

life expectancy in nature

0   **10**   25   50   75   100

weigh up to   70 kg (154 lb)

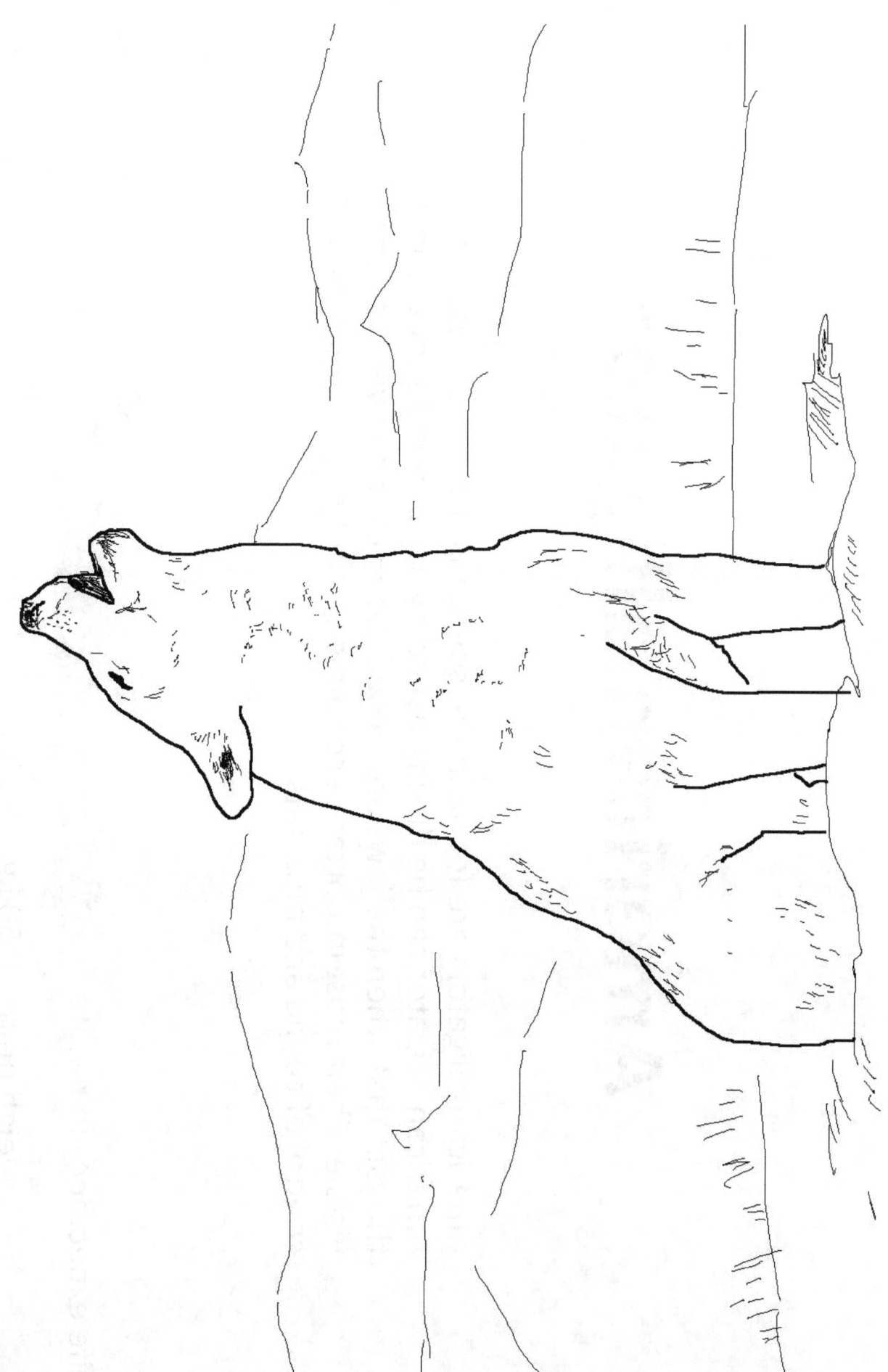

American alligator

American alligators are found in the southeast United States. the American alligator can be distinguished by its rounded snout, and by the fact that when the jaws are closed, none of the lower teeth are visible. Their most important economic benefit to humans may be the control of coypu and muskrats.

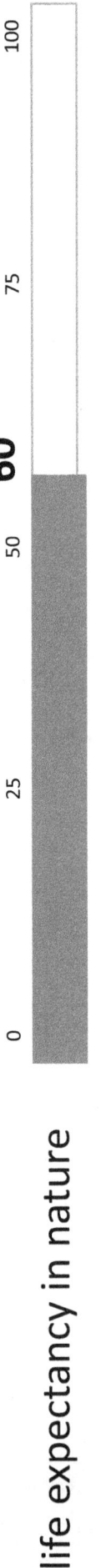

life expectancy in nature

weigh up to   50 kg (110 lb)

0   25   50   **60**   75   100

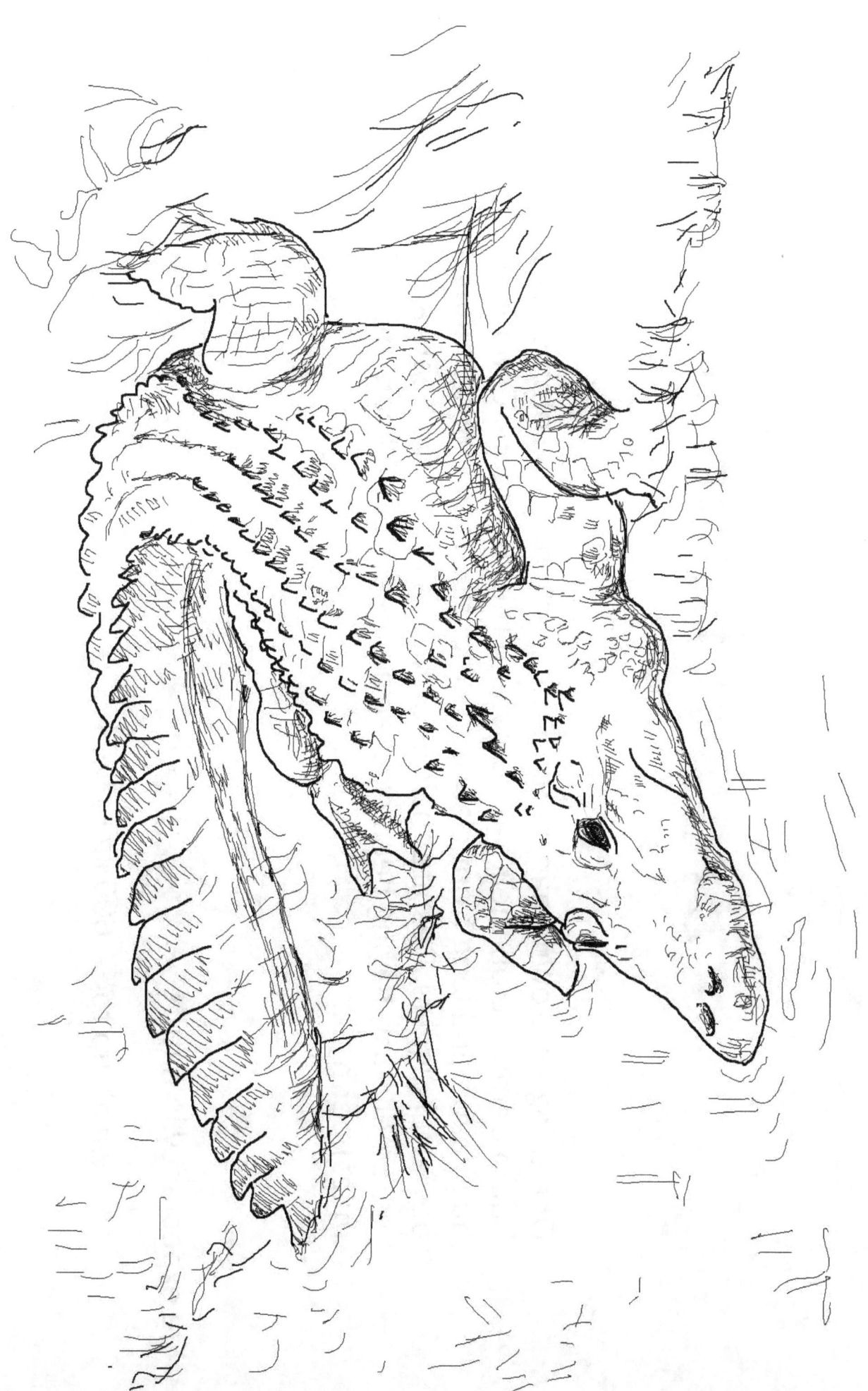

Brown bear

One thing all brown bears around the world have in common is a hump of muscle on their back between the shoulders. Combined with huge paws and long front claws, the muscles make these animals powerful diggers. Despite their enormous size, brown bears are extremely fast, having been clocked at speeds of 50 kilometers (30 miles) per hour.

life expectancy in nature

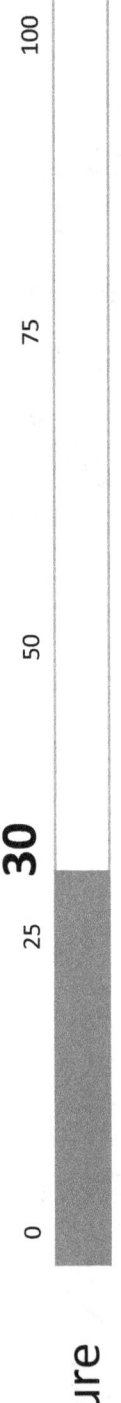

0   25   **30**   50   75   100

weigh up to   600 kg (1320 lb)

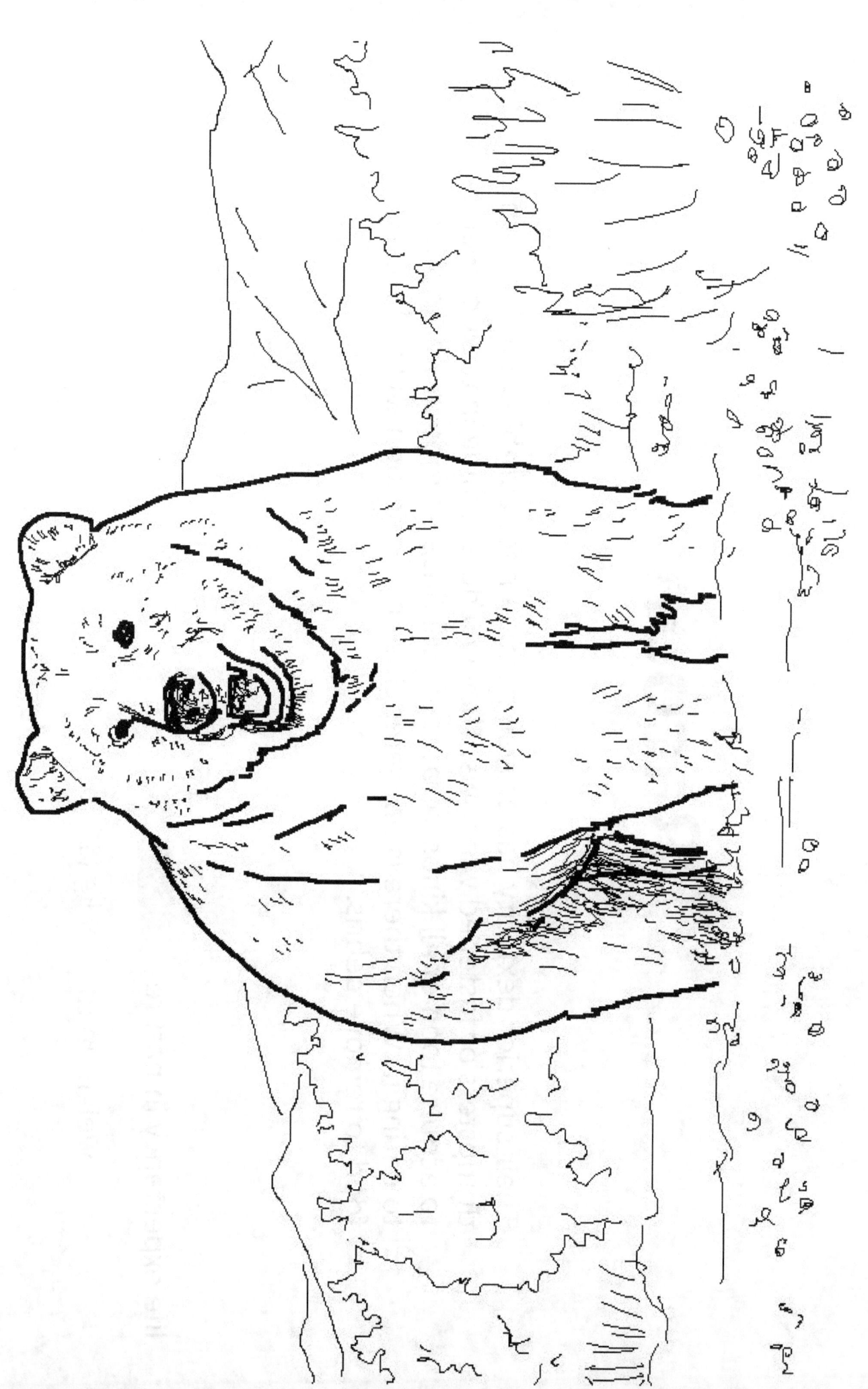

Racoon

Their superior dexterity has proved no match for combination locks on dumpsters or fastened windows. They will do anything in their power to acquire food of all kinds. A raccoon will rinse its food in water prior to eating it. When there is no water close by, a raccoon will still rub its food to remove debris.

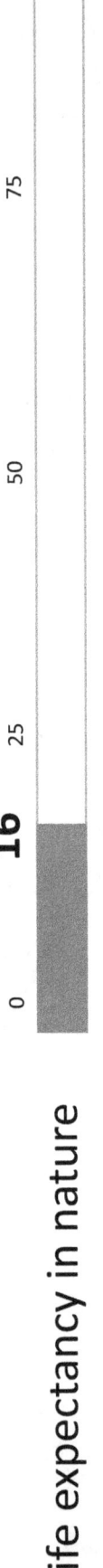

life expectancy in nature

16

0   25   50   75   100

weigh up to   9 kg (19 lb)

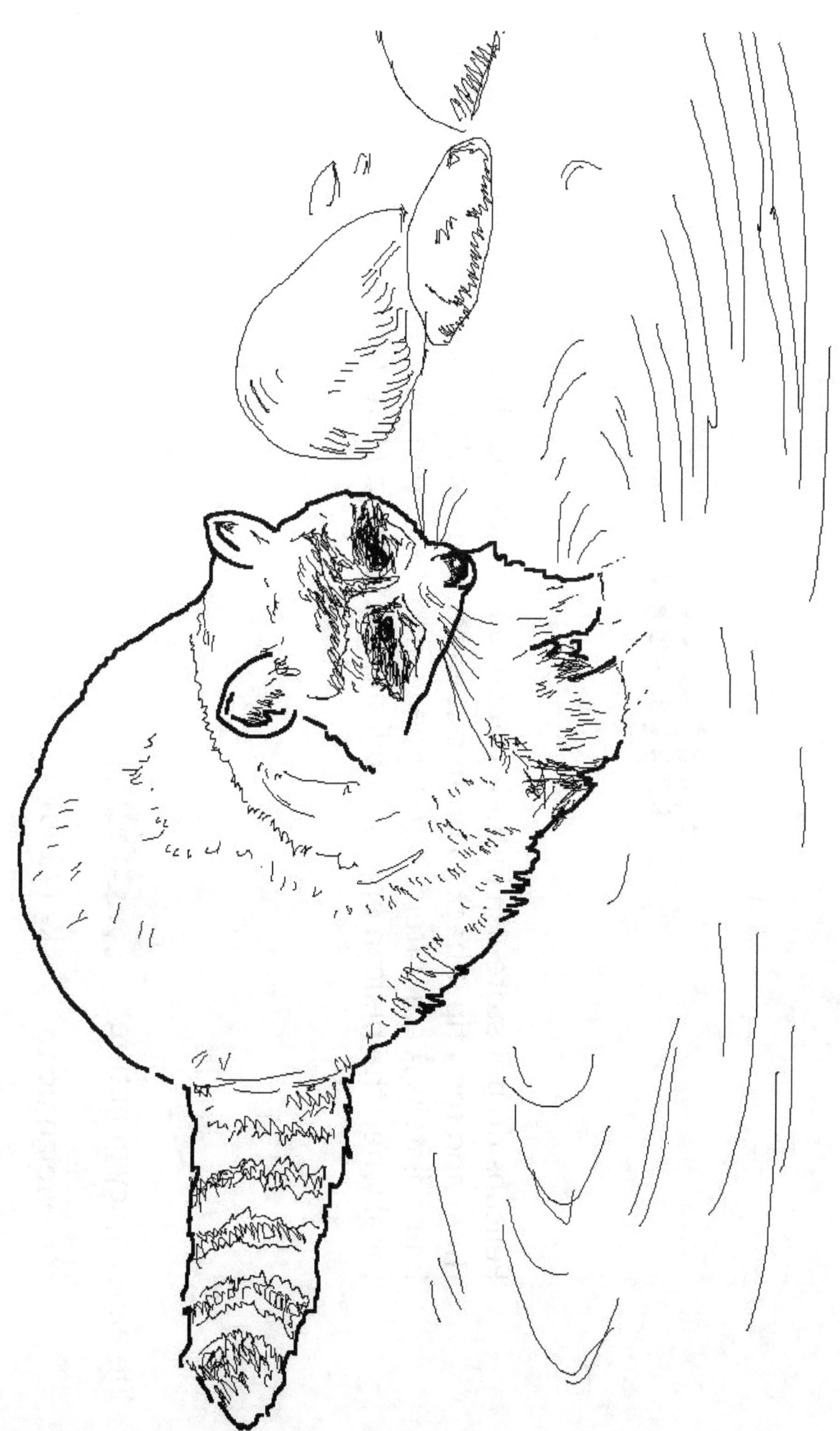

Pelican

Pelicans do not store fish in their pouch, but simply use it to catch them and then tip it back to drain out water and swallow the fish immediately. A gull often sits on a pelican's head, trying to steal a meal when the pelican opens its bill slightly to empty out the water

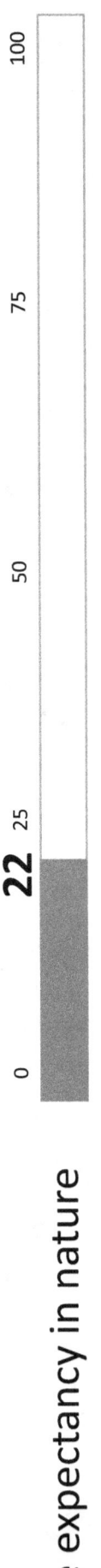

life expectancy in nature

0   22   25   50   75   100

weigh up to   5 kg (11 lb)

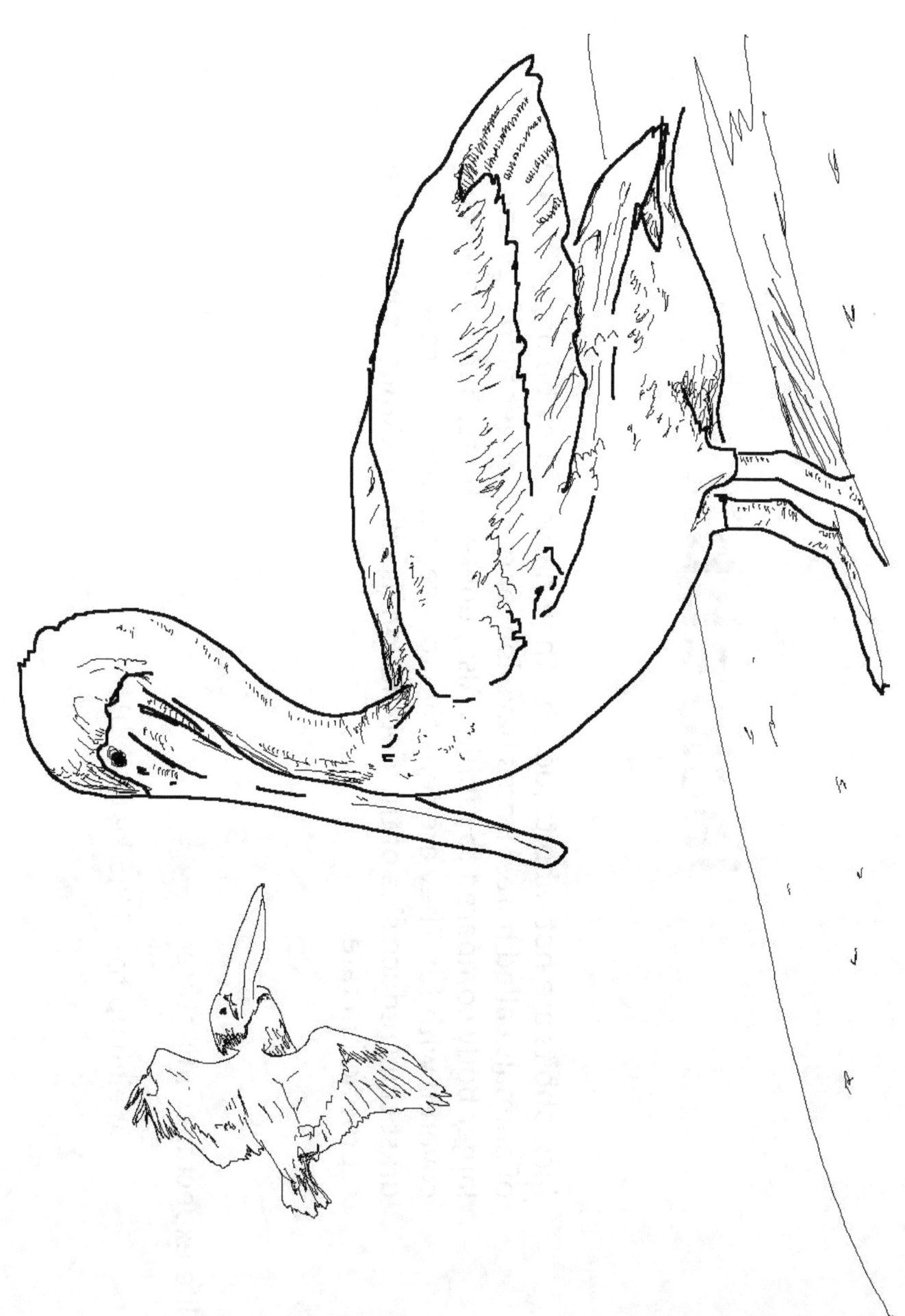

Jackrabbit

Jackrabbits are not rabbits (despite their name). They belong to group of animals called hares. Hares have longer ears, longer hind legs and larger body compared to rabbits. Also, unlike rabbits, hares are born covered with fur. They are sensitive to diseases which occasionally drastically reduce size of the population. Luckily, jackrabbits have high reproduction rate.

life expectancy in nature   **5**

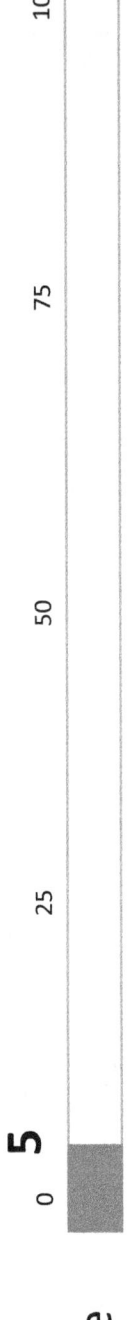

0   25   50   75   100

weigh up to   3,5 kg (7,7 lb)

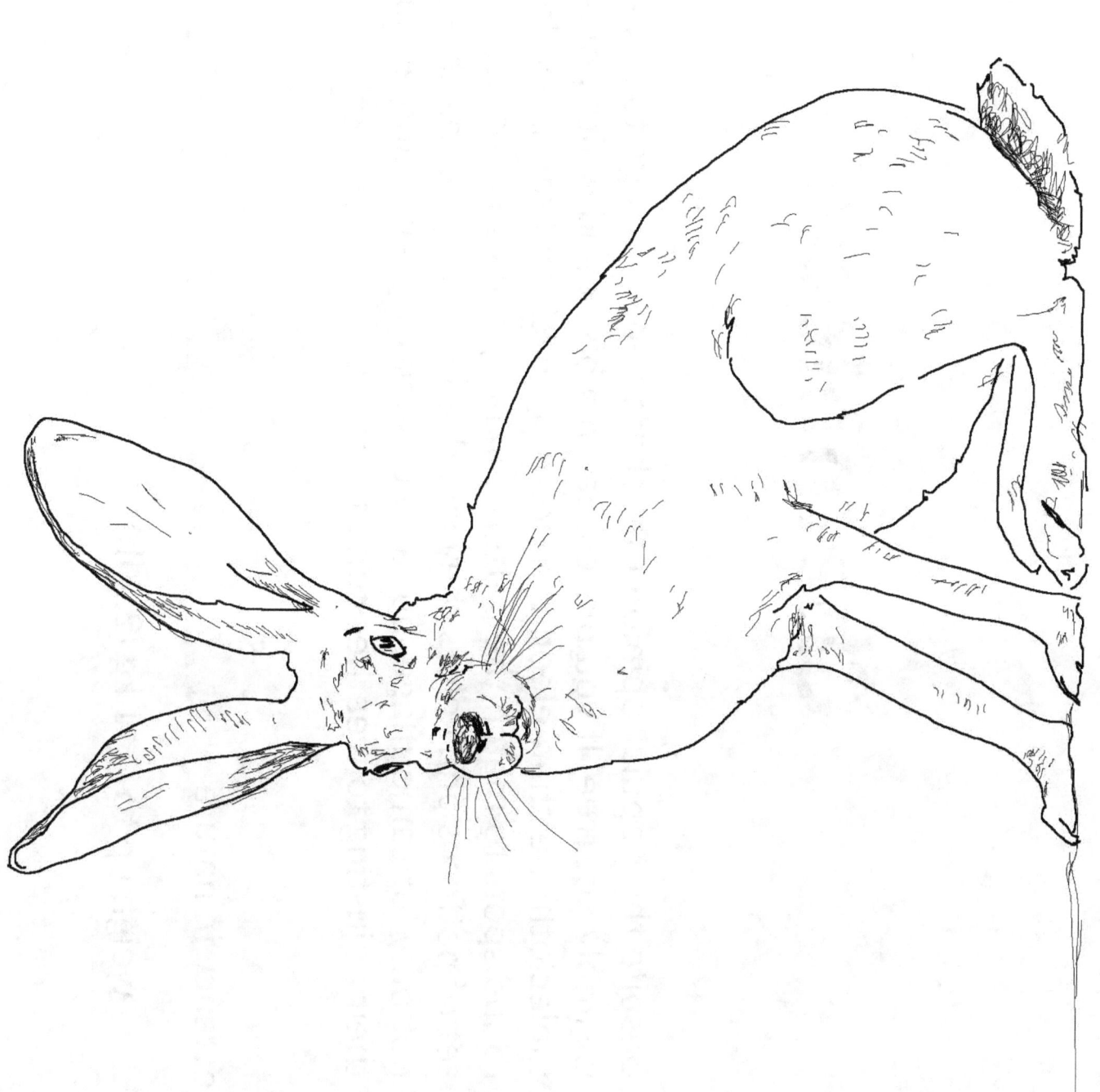

Chameleon

Despite the popular opinion that chameleons change to any color, that is simply not true. If you place one on a black and white polka dot tablecloth the chameleon will not turn black and then develop white round spots to match the pattern! In fact, each species has a certain set of patterns and colors they can display. Chameleons change color not only for camouflage, but also to social signaling and as part of their adjusting to weather conditions.

life expectancy in nature

5

0   25   50   75   100

weigh up to   1 kg (2,2 lb)

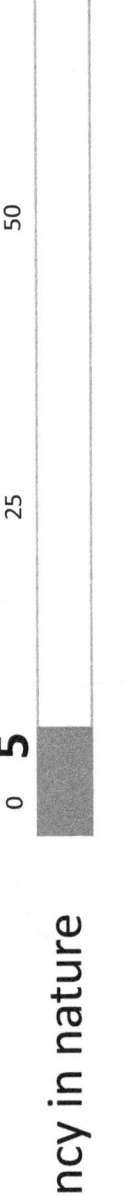

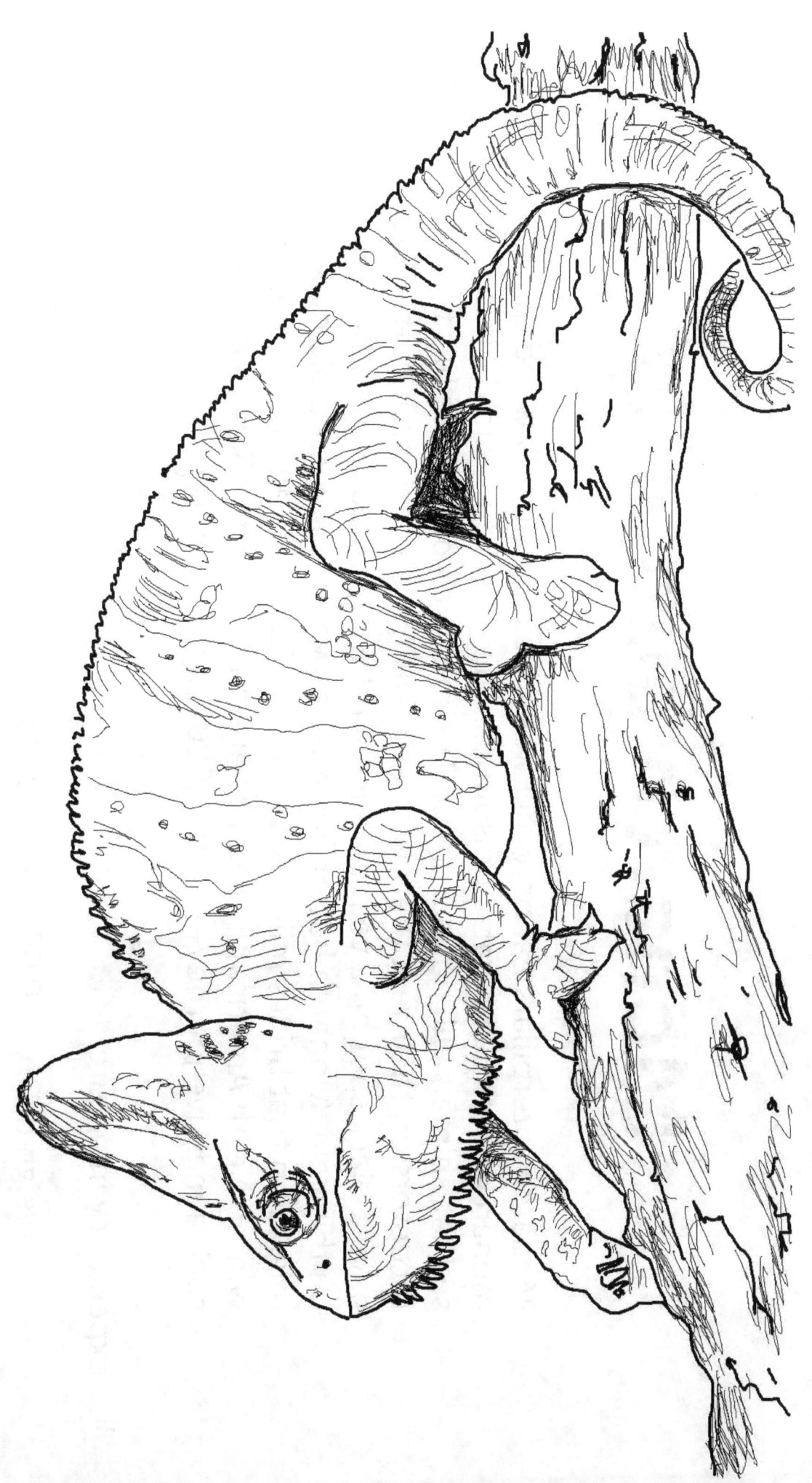

Monarch butterfly

Monarch caterpillars eat only milkweed leaves. The milkweed that monarch caterpillars eat is poisonous. The poison stays in their bodies so that animals will not eat them. The monarch butterflies has tiny receptors on their feet that they taste with. Male monarch butterflies have a black spot on a vein on each hind wing. Females have no spots on this vein. Monarch butterflies are known for the incredible mass migration that brings millions of them to California and Mexico each winter. North American monarchs are the only butterflies that make such a massive journey— up to 5,000 km (3,100 mile).

life expectancy in nature

0 **1**   25   50   75   100

weigh up to   0,001 kg (0,002 lb)

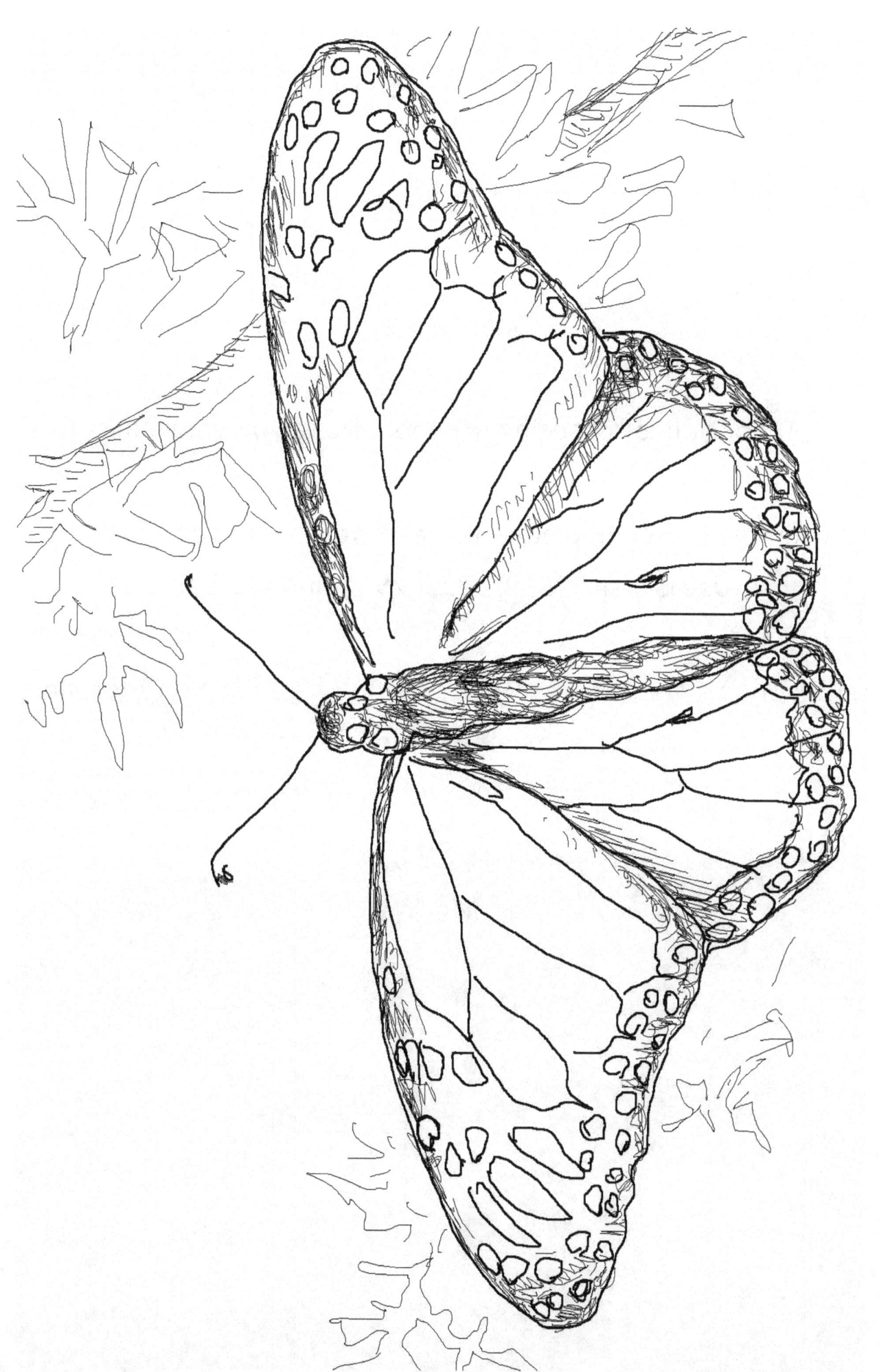

Dear Reader!

Thank you for choosing my book! Hope you enjoyed it!

If you really liked it, please, **leave a short review on Amazon!**
Use ISBN # 9781079225525 to find this book

Check out my website http://21centurywritersclub.com/ for more
books by me and my fellow writers!

See ya,
Mark

SEARCH MORE COLORING BOOKS

Book Series: Animal Planet

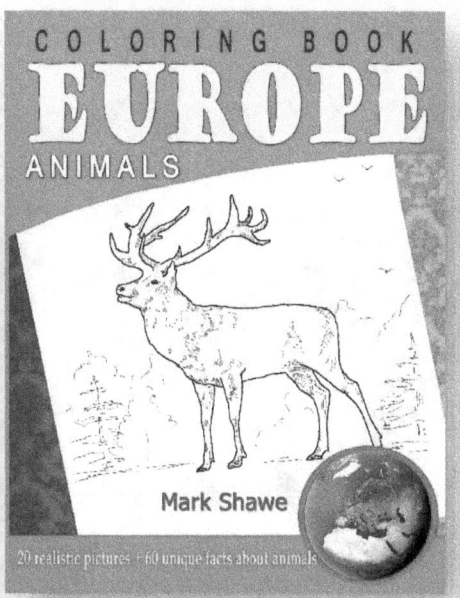

Animals of Europe

ISBN # 9781079222258

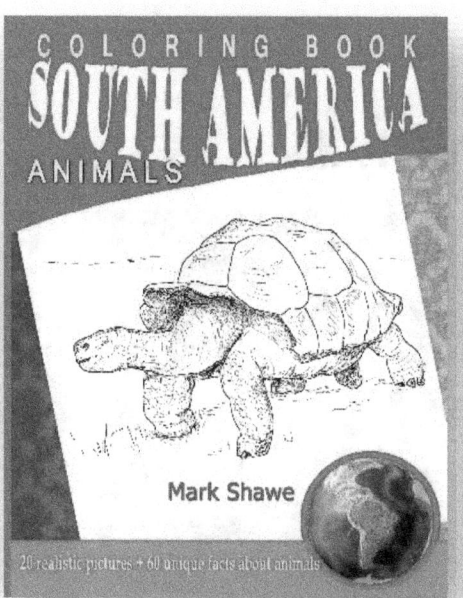

Animals of South America

ISBN # 9781079222920

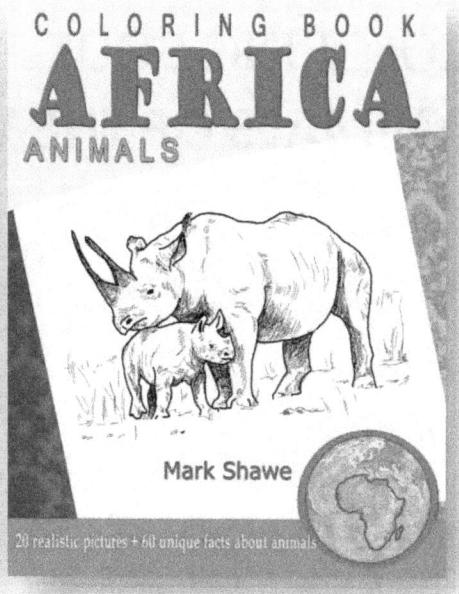

Animals of Africa

ISBN # 9781079227536

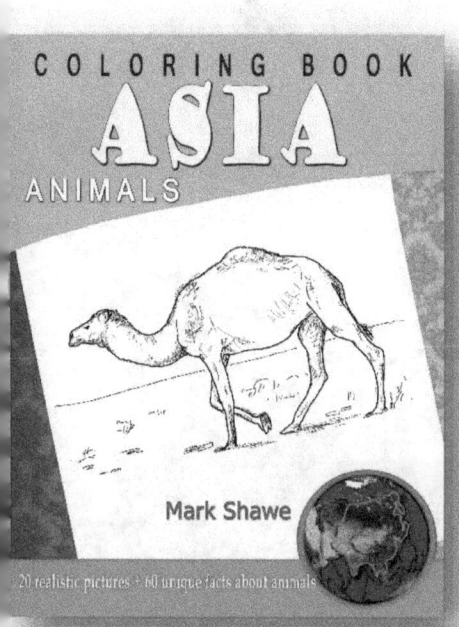

Animals of Asia

ISBN # 9781079224740

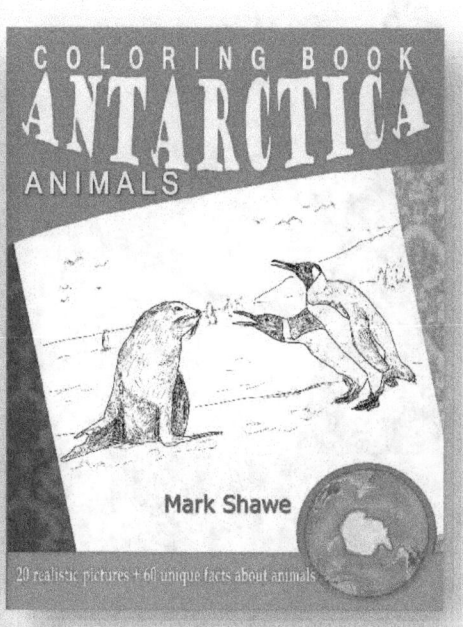

Animals of Antarctica

ISBN # 9781079225969

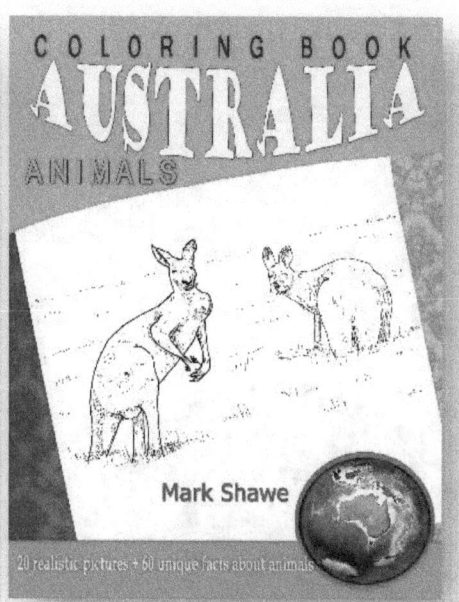

Animals of Australia

ISBN # 9781079226393

SPECIAL EDITION

COLORING BOOK:

ANIMALS OF THE WORLD

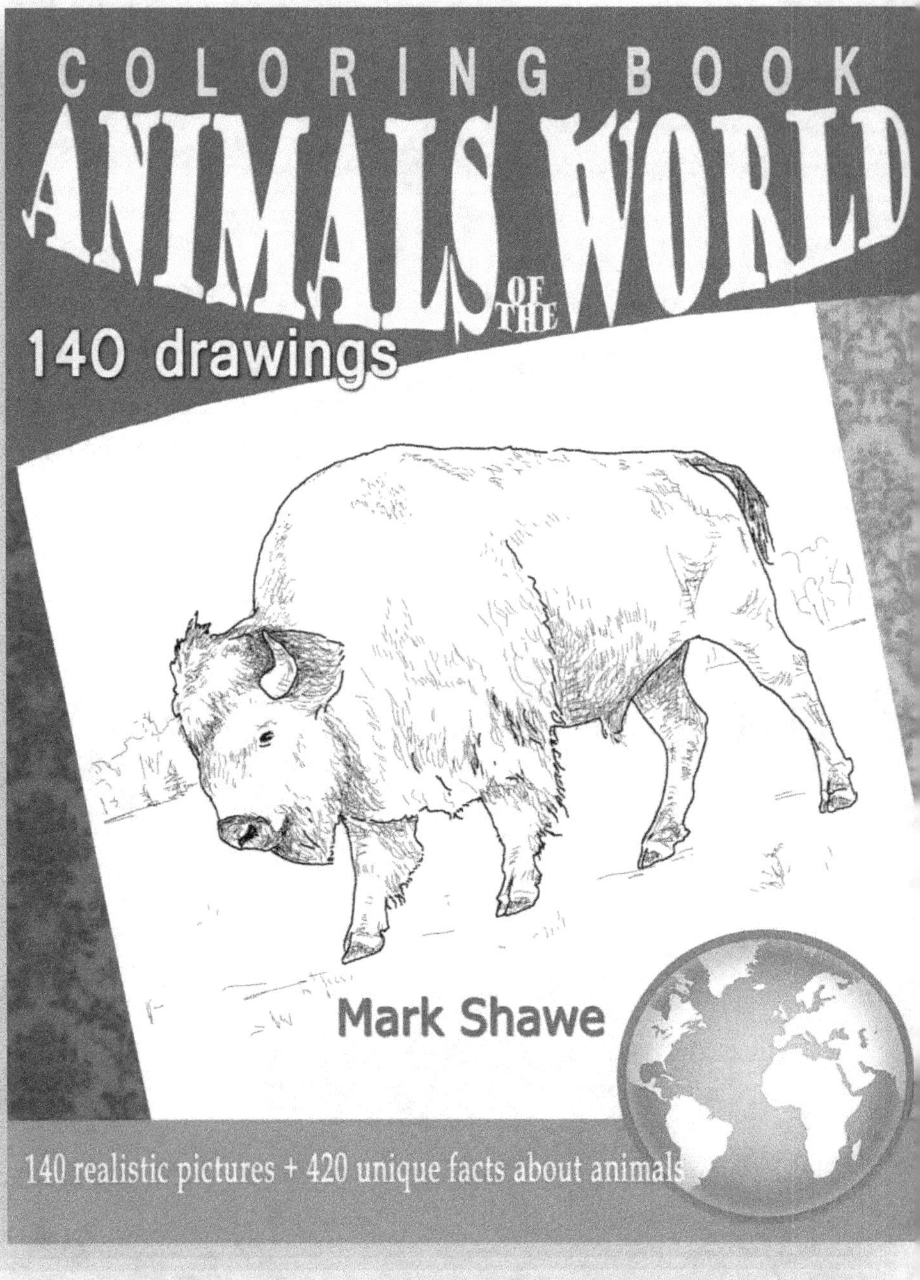

140 original realistic full-page images of wild animals of the World on single-sided sheets to prevent bleed-through

420 interesting unusual facts about the animals

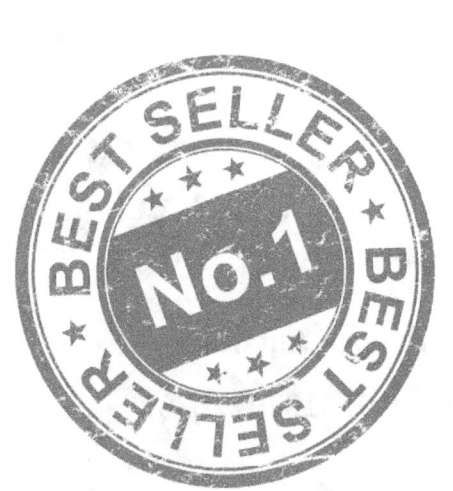

ISBN # 9781079226799

Book Series: Animal Planet